For Those
Who Will Come
After!

For Those
Who Will Come
After!

by Morgan Dalphinis

Karia Press

For Those Who Will Come After
Collected Poems (1968–1985).

First published in 1985 by Karia Press.

Front and back cover photographs by Lance Watson.
Cover design by Buzz Johnson.
Typeset by Karia.
Book design and layout by Buzz Johnson.

ISBN 0 946918 10 4 Pb.
ISBN 0 946918 11 2 Hb.

Karia Press
BCM Karia
London WC1N 3XX
United Kingdom

Printed in Great Britain by
Whitstable Litho Ltd., Whitstable, Kent

Contents

II. Conflict

III. Africa

For
Ernesta,
Audel,
Lilith,
Betty,
Sherman,
Louise,
and Joe.

Acknowledgements

Some of the poems published in this collection have been previously published in *Colleges Poetry,* London, 1972, the magazine of the *Africa Society,* School of Oriental and African Studies, University of London, 1976 and 1977, *Anthologie de la Nouvelle Poésie Creole,* Paris, 1984, *Caribbean Quarterly,* Jamaica, 1985 and *Caribbean and African Languages,* Karia Press, London, 1985.

The opinions expresses in this collection of poems are mind alone and do not in any way reflect those of any of my past or present employers.

Morgan Dalphinis
July, 1985

I: Innocence

The Plant

Spiraled
The webbed leaves,
To mingle the air,
Bound the extremities of their
Being.

Long lovely the lush,
Cascades of glistening green,
Which mingle me
The tangle of your
Being.

Sliding Ice

You would never guess, my friend
That visions are so simple;
That in this sliding block of ice
Which slowly forms a pool of water,
All thought of time, of space
Is mocked:
For ice is water
And water is ice,
Water is rain
And rain is vapour,
Vapour is cloud
And cloud is sky,
Sky is space
And space is time,
And time, is time is evermore!
And as it is all so simple,
I dare you to laugh!

Sunset

I walk along the road,
The sun flings his glory on my face,
Black buildings gilded by his embrace,
And me suddenly happy, suddenly calm.
His love lies gently at this time,
When he has shed his holy strength of day
And begs our love in acclamation
Of the glory in his death.

A Walk

As we went along the long lonely lane,
Where silence so steeps the air
That you cannot hear
The trembling of the fox in his lair.

I hold your hand and
Watch the autumn leaves change to green,
I watch your dead eyes and
Yet hope you can understand,
The silence which is man,
The acceptance that makes him
Master and slave entwined.

Song of the Old Man

Ah that we were young and lovely then,
And hearts in dreams weaved out
Life with dreamers dreams untold.

Sad, now I am old and cold,
And bitter black
The bareness of my heart.

Voodoo Child

I am the Voodoo child,
Beneath the snake's smile,
As I dance, move
Sense inscensed
Beneath the eyes of
Voudun[1],
Snake, charmed
Creator god of my people.

---

1.   The ancient religion of the Ewe, Fon and Yoruba of West Africa. In Saint Lucia it became a term for herbal medicine and witchcraft.

Ananse

Spider man,
Ananse[1] man,
Come man,
From sky man,
To earth
Man,
—Spider
In your wisdom.

---

1. The spider-trickster hero of the Twi/Fante of Ghana and of their
descendants in the Caribbean, particularly Jamaica.

Oh Sun

I salute you oh sun,
Free spirit,
Giving without asking returns,
Like God,
Like life itself,
I salute you oh sun.

The Trees

The trees, they twisted in the dark,
Their flesh convulsed in pain for breath,
And twiggy fingers cracked in blood;
Like old frightened hands that grasped for death.

You would not think they'd ever lived,
So cold, so black in death they seemed!
Like fallen victims where earth and sky embraced;
Who losing, fought vainly for their lives.

And though we may watch without involvement
They still remain so crushed in a fire;
Of blood, of love; a holy ghost in gloom,
And still asked reasons for their doom.

And I am dumb, numb —
Cannot answer; nor why, nor where or when
But echoing ask their question:
Why are we caught like rabbits so?
Held, fixed, fought, bought and martyred
For our breath!
Proclaimed in pain, in fire and in power
Chalices to the tasteless lips
Of indifferent gods!?

Wind

Burn these leaves
Within the passion of their own rustling.
Love this lust,
This mad rushing
Loving of these trees,
As their arms kiss
Ebb and flow the love between them.

But the wind
 Winding in a wirl,
Burning in the brown gold of the leaves,
Was at once involved
And lonely to this loving.
So he flew and blew his
Might to space,
As if to chase an endless race
To some new love,
From some new leaf to slither
Into space,
And bind from planets one to all
The universe within the
Warmth of his embrace.

Fingers

The hands and fingers of trees
Are many-shaped.
At times, direct
And straight in icicles of bark
They stand.
At times thick, fat, sausage-thick,
Clumsy and immovable.
But at times as if to beguile the dancers
Thin and reaching hands,
The hands and fingers of some
Single tree
Will touch upon eternities
No human mind can reach.

Spring

Yet darkness reigns the sky,
Men,
Former dead
Of winters dread.
Trees,
All cradled in the former
Dungeon bosom of the earth,
All feel the first spring shudders
Of awakening.

Spring-bound,
They rise to make,
Take, break
The dew-bound darkness
Of earth.

Yet still the cold clouds coil,
As if to finally deny
Any parody of birth.

But no,
Spring-broken
The clouds break,
Blue untortured skies reveal
As if in sudden sadness,
The gladness, of a mad
Spring morning
Earth.

The Dykes

Two dykes thrusting through
Earth,
Pillars forging full might up to
Sky,
Forcing all thoughts to throng
Upward.
Power without force,
Dynamic pillars of fire,
Tongues that throng with
Earth's volcanic thrust,
Heaven-ward.
Testimonies to nothing,
For and of
Nothing!
Such children of another age,
Another temperament
—A younger and more violent earth,
Such titans will not be soon
Forgot.

The Leaf

Yet
To die
The leaf shudders,
River below
Cries,
Its own wanton bosom
Begs
The body of the leaf:

Ah you my friend
One moment gone
A promise made
Mere reflection
Of the river:

She sighs
As if her wish may be denied,
Yet no ...
Some magical eternity breaks
The bud blood of the leaf:
Bespeckled,
Dew-eyed.

Yet to die
This prisoner falls,
Mingling
Down, down, down;
Ah yet to die.

But yet the life,
Yet the nimble
Un-numbered
Sun-dawned
Days;
Yet before this broken time

Ah yet to live:

Crying in the ecstasy of rain,
Living this ecstasy of pain,
Yet changing green,
Yellow
Brown
To make wonder the magic mystery,
Crying from change to change:
Ah yet to live.

The Sky Brother

Dark in the sky a shape recoils,
As if condemned in clouds to dance
An endless mindless trance
Of form: a web in which its flesh can coil.

But even fated thus he should recoil forever,
Lost: a ship of clouds upon eternal skies,
He can never escape the earth from which he flies,
And chained to earth remains: a mockery to his
    splendidness.

And even he is not alone in spirit,
For from the ageless dungeon earth
Primeval echoes call in endless birth,
Of tress, birds men and winds
Their claim of him as brother.

And we are all condemned, they call,
And all of us are fixed to fall
A point, a time a space
Of earth: a call in which the spirit flings.

The Angel

Before memories are doomed to the deep,
Steeped in the sediments of time,
A phantom calls
Not yet resolved;
For emblems of the mind dissolved.

But should I say this apparition spoke!
Would I be accused possessed?
Was such a sight, such a being!
For mere human vision meant?

"From a nameless kingdom of I have come," said he,
"I, king and kingdom of that air,
Soul of both sea and man;
Where humming bird to humming bird sings
Cuchendoed to the blowing breeze.
There angels twist among the palms,
And flood their souls in seas
Surrounding on every side!

At that, his words, the man,
The vision left.
But woven in my window then,
It seemed a web
Where space and time revolved.

He seemed to fly,
Oh high on high!
Deeper and deeper fled,
Slid upon waterfalls of air
Flying, facile in his element,
Seraphim to his own wonder.

He then dived and dipped his wings in sun,
Deep down deep,
Till pyred in a sea of light;
Like a bursting phoenix broke,
And spoke of words
That spoke of nothing but of song.

And as if such singing were enough,
A rift closed up,
Window became window,
Time and place:
These barriers closed all perceptions of his illusioned face.
But dreamers say they've seen him once,
And dying men but twice
That still I know,
And in nothing know
A grain of sand a wonder!
To thee the seraph of the sky.

The Warrior

Proud, steadfast the gleaming
Bronzen iron warrior stands.
Oiled in lions blood,
Fresh
Each tendon is ready,
Everything at one with earth:
The sweet morning-dewed woman.

Here he stands, spear glinting in the dawn,
Untouched, untainted, uneducated
Clean!
Beware my friends
Beware;
His time again will come,
The subtle sweet setting sun will crown him once more,
Again free, again
Man.

I am a Poet

Beyond my Negritude,
Beyond my white attitudes:
     I am a poet.
Above my loves,
Above my hates:
     I am a poet.
Above my life,
Beyond my death:
     I am a poet.

I Want to be Born Again

I want to be born again again,
So my soul may arise from a dark pit,
Over which black vultures swoop.

"I want to be born again,"
The dying soul screams:
"True, I know I am dying
True I know I am cold
And bitter in death's agony."

"But an insight deeper than my life:
The principle that calls
The phoenix to its pyre,
Stampedes the elephant to its tomb,
With a little voice tells me:
I can be born again."

So ferry me to Styx's dark stream,
Let me slide along the fearful walls
Where the soul's last amputated screams
Become a sigh ...
For I want to collapse with a thud —
Fall,
Be broken —
Shredded,
Decompose into the pit
Where the elephants' tusks become tombstones,
The phoenix dies within its ashes,
The scorpion stings itself
And dies within a ring of fire,
The pregnant woman screams
As the stern surgeon approaches with his knife,
But let me be born again,
Past these terrors,
Past these pains,

Past such fears that will kill forever.

Let me go calmly to my death,
Where the scalpel separates
A bloody birth to life —
The pregnant mother dies,
The ashes fall,
The gloried phoenix lifts its wings in birth,
So that my soul from this pit may
Arise
Slowly but explosively
In some pleasured agony burst into life —
A spring-born flower on a grave.

On Black and White

Time to forget these kings,
These gods of black and white.
Time to forget these rings,
That sap our strength and might.

Are we mere slaves and saviours
Of our skins
Or was man made for higher laws?
And fancy flung on higher wings?

A new universal dawn has broke
And mocked us in our games.
Time to forget these games,
Playthings for black and white.

The Last Romantic

Now quick my love before the summer dies
And like a dying lust, for winter cries,
Before I'm mourned an old and tattered thing
A love in words to you I bring.
I'll sing a song of promised love
As if it were the quiet musings of a dove,
And build you a bower of my dreams
Upon whose webs I'd weave the love of kings.
And there mid streams of dancing feet,
Beneath the whirl of birds' weilded wings,
We would like children make a song
In words not taught at school!
In plaints, in pities and in sighs
And gaze upon the splendours of star-spangled skies.

The Crucifixion

Must this man chance,
Dare that jibbering dance,
And from that unholy gibbet glance
That mad desire:
The hallowed nimbus of the cross.

Must he awake again,
Some yet-forgotten pain
Of stretching a bleeding hand
To caress a crooked nail
Which waits to hide
Behind some humoured, human smile
To beg the crucifixion of his being.

No!
Let him sleep,
Towered inside himself
And ring a river to a sea
Encompassing:
Tied to his own flesh,
Fleshed to his own dreams,
His own dancing:
These dying living chords of
Being.

Let sea moat tower,
Poetic yet
Let his word lash the waves,
Let him kill as he has
Been killed
Let him drown as he has
Been drowned.

Yet see, but see
Some lonely broken rider,

Horsed upon the madness of the waves
From this same bleeding soul direction begs,
Demands the re-incarnation of its light
From the bleeding desert of his being.

The waves lash upon themselves,
Receding to an ecstasy of calm.
A tower crumbles
And dust sings
The singing of such balm.

Let there be peace
The heaving sky sighed:
And there was peace.

The bosom of living laughed
Blooming the beauty of a being
Mad in an eternity of passion,
Loving,
As he could love,
Giving,
As he could give,
Yet silent as eternity commands,
Dumb as wisdom demands.

Earth-Bound, Earth Damned

Some distant clouds retract,
Their own loves enact:
Watching their heavenly frolic,
The sunlight, their love
Retracts.

Some long lonely tree,
Earth-bound,
Earth-damned,
Solemn:
Bounds up to join the play,
Yet,
Ah no!
Fingers too short,
Too clumsy to grasp them.

Some puddle beneath,
Dark in secrets,
Reflects in its own frolic,
Their frolic.

Mirror of their own mirrors,
Earth
Air
Sea
Sky
Love of their own loves,
All!
Mirrors in mirror reflected,
Lover from lover,
Retracted.

The Season of Revenge

'There will be war from generation to generation...'
The hot Saharan sands
Bosom forward,
Timbucktoo moves three miles back.
January now, Harmattan[1]
Screams his dessicating course
South.
'In times of evil the lord shall send his cures in flood,
        or plague or fire...'
The sands accumulate in legions
Of black and vengeful bodies.
Sun cuts down on former desert desolation
To glitter on erect,
And new-born spears.
'To everything there is a reason and a season...'
South the warriors move,
Through selvas, savannah,
Brush, the Green Veldt:
Green grass flames,
In red blood beneath their feet.
'The Lord had warned Pharoah many times; the plague
        was now come...'
'Uhuru' the cry to 'Uhuru'[2] replied,
Blood for past blood to be paid,
Brother to brother cried,
'Revenge', 'revenge!'

1.   A cold and dessicating wind which blows from the Sahara into West
Africa.
2.   A Swahili word meaning 'freedom'.

The Rude-Boy Walk

Not to be ashamed,
Neath White eyes,
Of this jump-up,
Bump-up rhythmn of our walk.
For this rhythmn,
This dignity and essence of our being
Has moved empires with lances,
Made the ancient knowledge
Of the world,
Within this same rhythm,
This same styled brillance,
That lies not only in our bodies,
But within the essence of our minds.

Masks

Each man a mask,
Each mask a mind
That no one dares to look behind,
And 'tis not only fear that keeps
Our silent spirits still,
But foreknowledge
Acknowledged,
The mockery of all knowledge,
That in its steely limits binds
Emotion, spirit, love behind
Masked carcasses of the human mind.

The Call of Death

The hands beat back,
The drums speak back,
Bodies beat; touch,
Back:
The black dancers meet –
Coiled in the rays of
The sun's last blood
Together!
Together!

Slowly the calm night;
Falls ...
Before dawn;
Calls ...
Sun moves back,
Slowly becomes black,
Dark moves back to a
Black ...
Forever.

Children move ...
Back; soft:
Burrowing deep,
With hungry mouths,
Their mothers' breasts
Deep to safety ...
Deep to forever.

Voices speak,
In mouths without tongues ...
Dark jibbering skeletons
Knocking ...
Together?

Everything stops
We cannot speak,
Talk:
I the sad priest
Who absolves you:
Thief who forever
Steals the miser's gold.
And you:
Cripple, laughing at us all;
Crippled together:
Blindmen, madmen,
We are together ...
Blind, sad.
Perhaps all mad ...
Together!

Dark in a dusk
Moving back to a black,
Ever to a dark
Unknowable forever:
There where hands do not touch,
Love is not mingled in a corrupting desire,
Lips dare not speak of death,
Where we are the dead
We the dark black drums
That call each other together:
Together! together!
Back to a black
Unknowable forever.

Poet in Impotence

Thirsty, the mind crackles,
Caked in a sickening dryness.
'Yet' — the wise men's mocking words
They haunt me —
'No good work of words
Quick becomes composed
By men of dried-out minds.'

'For those, though made of flesh,
Who toy with words,
To exchange for flesh
Fleeting visions of the spirit:
They need blood,
Lagoons of rich earthy blood
To flood dried
Spirit — aspiring minds!'

But to feel empty, hopeless
Fully fleshed, yet bloodless
To be left, hopeless, bloodless
And alone
Alone in a vacuum!

So quick to try and arm myself in power
Strength-power,
Mind-power
Word-power.

But where?
On what points, conflicts
Does the mind find strength
To conquer the strange limboed heights
Upon which all such power explodes?

Perverse exhuberance to claim such
Desired conquest,

As service to a God,
Yet slavishly deny there is a God:
No hope, no heights of power,
Nothing,
— Here twists to
Nowhere!

So near the devils hand I'll dance
In rings of closed spells magical,
Perversely hoping there to retain
Immutable firm faith of a fixed mind.

Useless!
The mind twists wide,
Long along bent roads, rails, highways:
Power locked in flaming tongues,
Inhuman jive of a steel piston,
Sharp shrill points squeeze in an
Incestuous anguish,
— Only a match and my mind may
Well explode!

Words

Passive, the poet worms beneath their power,
Insensed incestuously by their inherent anguish:
Words!

Never to leave a heaving mind:
Each one ever-eager
In its pregnant urgency to be born:
Words!

Quick the moments now return —
Gulls cry
— A thousand poetic gulls screaming their
Message across the sky:
Words!
The waves advance
— In squadrons the beaked waves smash the shore:
Words,
I see two headlands with a river valley between
— The lapping thighs of a long-legged whore:
Words!

Oh word upon word!
From magic to magic!
Your majesties bring convulsive life
To the cold and factual negation of existence.

As we Change

As we change,
As sinew grows on bone,
Fat on flesh,
What and who do we become?

We are not as we used to be,
But, in our new found states
Who can tell what we really are,
Or what we can really be?

Your Love

The first embers of a new-born star
Your love
Your lips to mine,
Our hands entwined,
For once my selfish hands did not ask
Who gave, who took.

And such a gift,
To be born again in you
To find, new hands,
New arms, new strength
New faith,
Your love's new strength
Laps me like a god,
I emerge, purged of old evils:
An Agememnon from the sea
A Chalka on Zulu plains,
A phoenix fired by a human kiss,
Kinged, crowned and kingdomed by your
Love.

Who are You Now Brother

With all your black gods destroyed,
Where are you now brother?
With musungu's[1] blood raped into your veins
Who are you now brother?
Though the old gods have fallen
And our precious blood mixed,
The game remains the same:
Black versus white,
The facts lack poetry.

1. A Swahili word meaning 'white people'.

On Ideals

And who would seek to look at stars,
The mind alienated from human-kind
The soul, a creature of its own
Castled where no blood, no flesh, no mind
Can claim its brotherhood?
Who would do this
And call it beauty? Adoration? Hope?

I can only say that you are vain,
I tell such men, turn round, look out
Behind you a gun takes aim,
A revolutionary holds it with his finger,
It does not matter whom the finger belongs to:
Your lover, friend or brother,
The answer is the same —
They also had their dreams,
Their own visions of beauty.
But they were not of stars
But blood.
The human belly feeds on food, not words.
And only practiced ideals, not ones on stars
Will always pave the human way.

The Middle Distance

On the last day,
Sad trumpets of deathday,
The moon will turn to blood,
Waking skeletons laugh.
We will wait to die again,
To sleep before another death.

The dead skeletons of leaves,
Will die from brown
To awake dead seedlings in green.

But will there be peace
In a new birth,
Forewarned, perhaps, like all births
By the necessity of a coming
Death.
Are we again to die?

And why, why should
The gods of change, birth, death
Deal their dooms, and mark
Their toll upon us.

But it will happen,
We are already marked from birth,
Words seem useless,
Ink wasteful
To say anything.

But in the end of no end,
Change of no change,
Perhaps time may stop,
Distance, space not matter:
And there will be peace

In everything,
A middle-distance
Where no gods hold power
Over us.

Pain

Can we stand this wreck
Called pain, oh Lord
Was man made to have brain
Storms of intellect,
Yet forced to endure a body
Capable of pain.

Is this thy will,
To force our minds
Downward,
To care for a corpse's curse.

And Jesus,
Did he have to feel
Pain,
Should a man of his mind,
Mettle
Be crossed, spreadeagled
Cursed, corpse on wood,
With head forced
Sideward,
Downward
To earth,
To fall from mind to
Body,
To crucify his body to
His mind
For thy will, thy kingdom
And thy peace?

'In life, all things have their cost,
The body's cry,
The mind's lust,
One for the other must pay,
And any peace gained of a man's mettled mind
Is not excused the price.'

Beware

Beware the long ships,
Beware, beware
The men of pale-blue eyes.

London— A City

The tramp asks me for the time;
I walk past with a pretended indifference.
Heavenly God forgive us,
For we know exactly
What we do.

If Only She Would Come

If only she would come,
Now
While there is silence,
On this, God's day,
Sunday.
While the pavements have just been washed
By rain,
While trees slowly dry their limbs
In the wind,
Rustle,
All is calm
Peace ...
If only she would come
Now.

Re-Birth

Eyes that cannot express,
Lips and hands that die in distress,
All elements of earth, woman and the death of all desire.
I would wish now for cold lips, hands,
Love of stone, of death to take over the murder,
   destruction
And re-birth of me.

Actor

I should, oh blood of my heart,
Heart of my blood, be an actor,
A handmaid of my mind.
Where like a mad moving mirror,
I could dissolve in fantasies
New forms, new expressions.

Artist

The artist's hands seek to destroy,
His art, born from the destruction
Of the every-day world,
Moves to create, its own
World:
Like a scorpion the creative mind turns back,
Back upon itself,
Eager to find some logic
For its own birth.

And like the scorpion,
Awaits with poisoned mirth
The self-destruction of this same birth.

Better to Destroy

Better to destroy,
Better to be destroyed utterly:
The shattered ends of human nerves
Palpitating in their last life,
While we die, die,
And something else is born.
Something else of godly shape,
Of godly mould,
Unconscious,
Unknowing of itself,
More beautiful than us:
A nothingless in which
Eternity is the power,
Our bodies, minds
Our selves
Merely vessels,
Of eternity.

Ki Moun Mwen yé?

Ki moun mwen yé?
Ki sa zòt vlé?
Ki sa zòt yé?
Misyé madam!
Misyé madam!
Mwen di kwik!
Mwen di kwak!
Wavèt pa ni wézon douvan poul:
Si nou sé wavèt èk blan sé poul?
Ki moun mwen yé?
Ki sa mwen vlé?
Ki sa zòt vlé?
Mwen sav.
Yo sav.
Nou sav.
Denmen sé toujou zòdi,
Sa mwen fè atcwèlman menm
Sé pou denmen,
Moun kay wè,
An chay pa kay kopwan,
Sé sa mwen yé
Mwen sé moun denmen.
Denmen poul pa kay ni wézon
Douvan nonm.

Who am I

Who am I?
What do you want?
What are you?
Ladies and gentlemen!
Ladies and gentlemen!
I say crick!
I say crack!
The cockroach has no rights before the chicken:
If we are cockroaches and whites are chicken?
Who am I?
What do I want?
What do you want?
I know.
They know.
You know.
Yesterday is also today,
What I do right now
Is for tomorrow,
People will see,
Many will not understand,
That is what I am,
I am a person of tomorrow.
Tomorrow chickens will have no rights
Before men.

A Prayer for Gentleness

That the willing hands of the forgiver
Be gentle,
Gentle now.

That there be peace with the giver,
The lord
And the master.

Peace for the slave with the work,
And the work
With time.

For the frailness of human hands retract from pain,
And even in the splendours of crucifixion
The dolorous knot of human agony remains.

So work, slave, master, giver,
The forgiver,
Be gentle
Gentle now.

Soul on Ice

Soul on ice,
Ice on the human soul.
Some day the waters of this world
Will flow over the earth again.

Till then,
Till we are placed
In the power of a greater,
And more overpowering source.
Till then, out of place,
Out of context to each thing,
Persons, feelings, things;
In this free vortex we are lost
In chaos,
Chaosed to each other.

Till then,
As if our souls were on ice,
As if ice is on the soul,
We can know nothing of the world;
Let alone each other.

Twinned Spirits

Twinned and youthful beauty,
How can I tell one from the other?
Your yesterday's promise is now today's reality,
Your youth's dreams now in the bower of your love,
Your union so matched in this earthly shell,
May it mirror a deeper unity within,
A deeper love to grow steadfast
In tomorrow's trials,
Remain as true and deep in age,
As passionate and as fired in youth,
A summary you are twinned spirits,
Two love birds drinking from the same fountain
Of what is god-like and pure in us,
The best hopes of yours are
Ours all,
Like light bou.ding pure from twinned stars,
Sparkling, dazzling,
Your spirits to our spirits,
In one united love.

Ah! Beauty, Beyond the Telling of it

Breaking all self-embounded thoughts,
Wonder-like,
Waves propel,
Erode the silence,
Ebbing the inmost inlet of my mind.

Crash the thunder,
Wonder bound the element,
Caressing
Carves, god-like
Its own image from the stone.

Tears of knowledge,
Pain to witness
Such godly loving,
Bound from me
As the waters trickle from the stone
And trickle back to sea.

Yet slowly the stout, soul-bent old woman,
Years and tears dried out,
Traces
To retrace
Following my tears to sea.

II: Conflict

Far From You

Near the river,
As a woman,
As yourself,
I loved
You.
Far from the river,
Bourne
A vessel in the flood of life.
Far from you,
I can still love
You.

But carried,
Slowly carried
By time,
By water
And by space,
Slowly
So slowly,
Like a matchstick on a river,
These gods have ferried me,
Ferried you,
Slowly drowning our love in the flood:
Alas, alas
I am carried
Ferried,
Like the river
By the river,
Alas I am here crying,
Drowned in the river
By the river,
But far, so far
Far from you.

Iounaloa[1]

How long since I left Iounaloa's
breast,
How many years, how many seas,
How many deaths, rebirths
and deaths.

Did we not charm the skills of
the sea,
And travel from forest infested
South America,
To search for open areas?
Did we not always,
Fated to our love of movement
Only move on, move on
In hope of hope, in hope of
future paradises.

But so many travels my ancestor,
From then through Trinidad
To smaller and smaller islands
Till we arrived at Iounaloa.
But restless still we crossed
Our Carib sea,
To arrive at Nicaraguan and other shores.

And even then this restless need
for novelty has not stopped,
Now in England,
How long and how far
Have I left the sweetness of
Iounaloa's breast.

1. The Carib name for Saint Lucia.

The Bird

Not on iron wings shall this bird fly,
His feathers fling on silken winds;
Not fashioned by human hands that die,
His reeling soul he wields.

He, this king and kingdom of the air,
Betwixt the ether and the earth shall dare,
To cloak his spirit free,
In savage turmoil that is he.

And though the sky in spirit flings,
Damnation to the earthen origin of his wings,
This being shall not fall, neither to earth, nor sky;
Wings fastened to a call, so high,
Forged in the earth aura of his cry.

Together

We are together;
The murderer and victim
Commune before the knife falls down:
Together!
We are together;
The dying leaves of trees
Like flies stream down:
Together!
Loves that have come and gone:
Hands, kisses, lips, bodies
All back:
Together!
I love you a child once said.
I hate you said my brother:
Love, hate;
In time: the knife of life
Those feelings, words of sand,
Dust;
Forever, like all things
Seem twisted:
Together.

The Eye of God

Rain
Falling,
Strings structured from earth
To sky kingdom,
Trees mass up from earth
Giving width to sky
And earth's landscape.
— Vision of earthlings this
Small comparison to a universal view.

The eye of God, perhaps,
Would hold such things a speck,
Mere nothing, dried grain,
Nothing to think about...

Yet the eye of man,
Poor weakling man,
Lost to love Earth, this speck,
This fractured fragment of
Leaves,
Twigs,
Trees,
Blades of grass, from whose colour,
The blue sky creeps
To the Heaven — God's arms,
The eye of man with this immense
Yet little kingdom,
Can only in the mind fuse
In such poetic thoughts, a hope
Pattern,
Allusion to some love,
— Unity
Between the eye of God
And the eye of man.

Ghetto in the Soul

Barred the prison windows of this room,
Where poverty the jailer,
Keeps its black man-child prisoner closed.

In ghetto room also sits
Mother, the woman looks back, despairs:
Black woman re-sold again
Through the African chief's greed-greasy hands
To the slave-master's prostituting needs,
Through the black male slave's irresponsible hands
To Babylons in England, U.S.A. or Canada —
These, the bigger prisons,
Wherever slaves can shackle themselves
As servants, musicians, hotel-boys,
Their fool-white smiles breaking the wound
Of black faces
To utter the slave's heritage:
"Cann Ah!, Cann Ah help you Massah?"

Man, all these damn countries,
All these damn rooms,
The damn same
In which some cultureless, fatherless, institutionless
Black bastard wails
To a black mother's face,
As poverty fixes us in traps
For the vulture deprivation
To feed upon we,
Most unprepared, most innocent,
Most carrion,
Blacks.

But history, time, such moments of bitter knowledge
Teach their lesson well:
Black men children of the ghetto

Wait with guns, bullets, knives, brains
For the time to come,
For our black dreams
To become real,
For our black dawn to rise...

So, before the springtime of all this we wish,
We work, we learn,
We wait,
We study the order that must fall
— Within the houses of the white and rich,
Sipping cocktails with the black
I'm all right black brother bourgeois clique,
Having intellectual tea with the white liberal.

For the time to come
Will come,
And the dawn genesis of drums
Will sound,
And the soldiers black will rise,
Ready to kill,
Ready to die,
As blacks for blacks
— A Ghetto in their souls.

Tchébé'y Fò[1]

Greetings now on this day of your joy,
Now let every happiness be yours,
Leaving now your youthful zest,
For the firmer wine of adulthood.

Yesterday was winter dark, without light,
Yesterday was your struggle with only
Your courage as your friend.
Now, beyond the tears of yesterday,
Today's light shines brightly
Upon your new jewels of experience,
And founding your happiness on more
solid ground.

So now in joy we herald with the light of spring
The joy of love upon yourselves and on your daughter,
Remember you three have already
Founded what others still look to find,
So hold it hard,
Or in other words tchébé'y fò.

1. A St Lucian Patwa greeting meaning 'Hold on hard to life'.

Peter Moses

Peter Moses was born in Dominica in July 1945. He came
to England during the period that many West Indians
used to go there to (find) work (during the 1960s).

He used to do a lot to help West Indians in Shepherds
Bush, London, to become more aware of the history of
their country and how they were being marginalized by
British society.

While involved in this general work he began a system
which has had important influences on young West
Indians. This was the Supplementary Schools System to
educate young West Indians in Mathematics, English,
African History and Caribbean History every Saturday in
Shepherds Bush. The name of the school was the Marcus
Garvey Supplementary School. In the school, West Indian
teachers and trainee teachers, including the writer, all
helped to teach the pupils.

Peter Moses also used to teach; but his important
contribution was in organising the parents of the pupils.
Whilst doing all that, moreover, Peter used to organise
West Indian self-help projects: redecorating each others
homes, visiting the sick, collecting old clothes and giving
them to those who did not have any, and other projects.

One day Peter came to know that he had leukaemia,
but, despite this, he continued with his work. He did
other political work with other West Indian organisations
like Grass Roots. He continued to work.

We have the proverb: 'If you see your friend's beard
catch fire, throw water on your own.' (*Si'wè bab
kamawad'w pwi difé voyé difé asou sa'w.*) Peter was not
that kind of a person; if his friends or his people were
in difficulty, he would go and solve these difficulties
even when he himself was almost overcome by his own
problems.

He died in December 1972. We buried him. In April
1973 we organised a memorial festival for him. The money

collected at this festival was given to Fortuna, his wife, and Candice, his daughter.

At this festival I read the following poem which I wrote for him.

Gwendé pou Peter Moses

"Yon!"
Gwendé-a tonbé,
Twa gwan nèg¹ka jwé,
Wonm fò ka woulé andidan tèt yo,
Kon di yo kay fè
Zéklè avèk jòl yo.
Men gadé yon ti nèg,
Ti nèg,
Ti nèg,
An ti nèg ki pa avèg,
Ki ka gadé,
Ki ka èspéwé, pòv ich,
Pou sa i pa sav
Douvan syèl blé, lanmè blé
Bondyé.

Élas, élas, ki moun, ki moun
Pami zòt,
Ki
Té
Ka
Konnèt li?

"Dé!"
Nèg anlè bato,
"Dé!"
Nèg ka alé wè Langlitè yo,
Nèg ka koupé chimen èslav ankò,
"Dé!"
Vyé nèg ka bwè wonm yo,
Vyé nèg ka jwé gwendé-a,
Yo ka jiwé an ti nèg:
"Men sa ou vlé ti gason?
Sé bagay gwan moun isi-a,

Dice for Peter Moses

"One!"
The dice fell,
Three old West Indians[1] are playing,
Strong rum rolling in their heads,
Laughing
As if they would make
Lightning with their mouths.
But behold a young West Indian,
Young West Indian,
Young West Indian,
A young West Indian who is not blind,
Who is watching,
Who is waiting, poor child,
For what he does not know,
Before the blue sky, blue sea
Of God.

Alas, alas, who, who
Amongst you
Used
To
Know him?

"Two!"
West Indians on-ship,
"Two!"
West Indians are going to see their England,
West Indians are re-excavating the road of slavery,
"Two!"
Old West Indians are drinking their rum,
Old West Indians are playing dice,
They are cursing a young West Indian:
"But what do you want little boy?
This is the business of old (and respected)
People (going on here),

Bab mouton
Pa ka fè nonm."
Pòv ti nèg
Nèg jen,
Adjablès² andidan tchè'w,
Manman Glo³ anba pyé 'w,
Ki koté, ki koté 'w sòti,
Ki koté 'w ka alé?

Élas, élas, ki moun, ki moun
Pami zòt,
Ki
Té
Ka
Konnèt li?

"Twa!"
Gwendé-a tonbé,
Langlitè mèg twouvé 'w,
Hélé, tout nèg san plas,
Dézèspéwé andidan an lòt was.
Ayen pou di
Ayen pou fè,
Twa!
Twa!
Twa pa twa!
Andidan ti pak Brixton,
Andidan ti pak Wolverhampton
Yo ka jwé gwendé-a.
"Gadé an jen nonm
An ti nonm nèg kon nou,
Anou mandé 'y jwé gwendé."
"Men sa pa pou mwen", jen nèg-la di,
"Kous lavi twò vit,
Èk an bagay pa bon
An bagay ja pouwi,
An fwi ja gaté pou nou.
Gwendé pa kay édé mwen twouvé
Wézon poutchi."

A goatee (beard)
Does not make (you) a man",
Poor little West Indian
Young West Indian,
'Adjablès'[2] in your heart,
'Mama Glo'[3] under your feet,
Where, (oh) where have you come from,
Where, (oh) where are you going?

Alas, alas, who, who
Amongst you
Used
To
Know him?

"Three!"
Dice fell,
England West Indians have found you,
Cry, all West Indians without status,
Desperate amongst another race,
Nothing to be said
Nothing to be done,
Three!
Three!
Three by three!
In the small parks of Brixton,
In the small parks of Wolverhampton
They are playing dice.
"Behold a young man
A young West Indian like ourselves,
Let us ask him to play dice".
"But this is not for me", the young West Indian said,
The course of life is too quick,
And something is spoilt
Something has become rotten,
A fruit has become spoilt for us,
Dice will not help me find (out)
The reason why".

Élas, élas, ki moun, ki moun
Pami zòt,
Ki
Té
Ka
Konnèt li?

"Kat!"
"Kat, fè kat pou mwen doudou!"
Sé gwendé-a woulé,
Tchèk plas,
Tchèk koté,
Nèg ka jwé.
Men pou yon jen nèg
Tonné ka pléwé,
Zéklè pété,
Zonbi san zo palé,
Soukouyè[4] gwaté,
Syèl ka tounen wouj, wòz,
Nwè, blan, blan
Nwè.
Lwen dèwò lakay li
Lwen dèwò péyi 'y,
Andidan lanfè yo ka kouyé
Anglitè,
I koumansé sav ko 'y menm,
I koumansé sav,
Nwè, blan,
Blan, nwè,
Blan vlé tchwé nwè,
Men nwè, ou konnèt,
Vyé nèg yo vlé jwé gwendé.
Èk pòv piti nèg
Pòv piti ich Domnik,
I koumansé sav . . .

Élas, élas, ki moun, ki moun
Pami zòt,
Ki
Té
Ka
Konnèt li?

Alas, alas, who, who
Amongst you
Used
To
Know him?

"Four!"
"Four, make four for me (my) darling (dice)!"
The dice rolled,
Some place,
Somewhere,
West Indains are playing.
But for one young West Indian
Thunder cries,
Lightning bursts,
Zombies without bones speak,
'Soukouyè'⁴ scratches,
The sky turns red, rose,
Black, white, white
Black.
Far from his home
Far from his country
In the hell known as
England,
He bagan to know himself,
He began to know,
Black, white,
White, black,
White wants to kill black,
But black, (as) you know,
Old West Indians want to play dice.
And poor little West Indian
Poor little child of Dominica,
He began to know ...

Alas, alas, who, who
Amongst you
Used
To
Know him?

"Senk!"
Gwendé tou piti
Gwendé tout koulè,
Gwendé ka dansé anlé lavi tout moun
Lè Bondyé ka jwé . . .
Ti nèg
Ti nèg
Ou sav ou kay mò,
Ou sav ou ni an maladi
Ki nou pa pé djéwi pou 'w?
Ti nèg,
Ti nèg ki pa pé pléwé,
Ti nèg ki sa ou kay fè?
Pyès voudou[5], pyès fèy obiya[6],
Ni medsin Djolif[7] ni maji nwè
Pa pé édé 'w,
Pa pé sové 'w.

Élas, élas, ki moun, ki moun
Pami zòt,
Ki
Té
Ka
Konnèt li?

"Sis!"
Bondyé an syèl,
Nèg anba,
Tout ka jwé gwendé-a . . .
Moun ka vini,
Moun ka mò,
Ki sa pou di?
Ki sa pou fè?
Men avan lafen istwa sala,
Avan lòt ting ting bwa chèz,
Avan gwendé dènyé Bondyé té jwé,
Avan Moses té mò,
Moses té wè ki non 'y té bon,
Ki kon tout non Afwitchen
I té ni bagay dèyè 'y,

"Five!"
Dice so small
Dice of all colours
Dice dance on the lives of all
When God is playing ...
Young West Indian
Young West Indian
You know you are going to die,
You know you have an illness
That we cannot cure (for you)?
Young West Indian,
Young West Indian who Cannot Cry,
Young West Indian, what are you going to do?
No 'Voudou',[5] no 'Obiya'[6] leaf,
Nor Djolif's[7] medicine, nor black magic
Can help you,
Can save you.

Alas, alas, who, who
Amongst you
Used
To
Know him?

"Six!"
God in heaven,
West Indians below,
All are playing dice ...
People come (at birth),
People die,
What (is there) to say?
What (is there) to do?
But before the end of this story,
Before any other 'ting ting bwa chèz'[8]
Before the last dice of God was thrown,
Before Moses died,
Moses saw that his name was appropriate,
That like all African names
There was some (hidden) meaning behind it,

Menm kon Moses pami Jwif
I vini kon Moses pami nou
I twavay kon an chyen
Pou èdyiké ti
Mamay nou nwè
Pou sové tèt yo d'adjablès moun blan,
Pou sé ich nou pa pé
Sèlman èspéwé gwendé, wonm fò èk mové fanm,
Pou ich nou pé vwéman vini gwan nonm
Entèlijan.

Élas, élas, ki moun, ki moun
Pami zòt,
Ki
Té
Ka
Konnèt li?

"Sèt!"
Sèt! Sèt! Sèt!
Tchenbwa[8] nèg ka jwé gwendé:
Gwendé nwè!
Gwendé voudou!
Gwendé voudou!
Gwendé èslav!
Gwendé nou ka woulé,
Gwendé nou ka pwédyé:
Bondyé moun nwè,
Tchébé 'y tchébé 'y pou nou!
Tchébé 'y tchébé 'y an tjè nou,
Ek menen èspwi 'y Afwik pou nou:
Lumumba, Jackson, Fanon
N'krumah, Malcolm X, Peter Moses,
Tchébé gwan pwèt
Nou la,
'La pou nou!

Men élas, élas, élas, élas pou nou, pou nou
Ki
Té
Ka
Konnèt li.

Just like Moses amongst the Jews
He became like Moses amongst us,
He worked like a dog
To educate young
Black children
To save their minds from the 'Adjables' mentality of
whites
So that our children should not
Only hope for dice, strong rum and bad women,
So that our children may really become great and
Intelligent (men and women).

Alas, alas, who, who
Amongst you
Used
To
Know him?

"Seven!"
Seven! Seven! Seven!
West Indian 'Tchenbwa'[9] plays dice:
Black dice!
'Voudou' dice!
Slave dice!
Our dice are rolling,
Our dice are praying:
God of Africans,
Hold him, hold him for us!
Hold him, hold him in our hearts,
And bring his spirit to Africa for us:
Lumumba, Jackson, Fanon
N'krumah, Malcolm X, Peter Moses,
Hold, our high priest
There,
There for us.

But alas, alas, alas for us, for us
Who
Had known him.

1. *Nèg* in Patwa can be used neutrally as a term of address. Compare Black American *Nigger* and Caribbean English Creole *boy* as other examples of negative terms used positively in the speech of Africans in the Americas and the Caribbean.

2. A woman with one cloven hoof who, in Patwa mythology, entices men to their death by luring them to jump over precipices in their bids to gain her favour.

3. A woman who lives in the sea and rivers and who, in Patwa mythology, entices men to their death by drowning in their bids to gain her favours.

4. A vampire-like creature who inhabits human form by day but, by night, can turn into an animal or a flying creature in order to suck the blood out of animals such as cows and sheep, as well as out of human beings.

5. The ancient religion of the Ewe, Fon and Youruba of West Africa. In Saint Lucia it became a term for herbal medicine and withcraft.

6. A Twi/Fante term refering also to herbal medicine and withcraft. The item has the same meaning in Saint Lucian Patwa.

7. A deceased Saint Lucian herbalist of fame in Saint Lucia and neighbouring islands. The name Djolif itself may be a corruption of the West Senegalese ethnic group the Wolof/Djolof.

9. A Carib term meaning 'witchcraft' in both Carib and Saint Lucian Patwa.

Moses

"And the Lord said to Moses, 'Go in, tell Pharoh. . . Let my people go. . .' " –
Book of Moses.

I have been the viewer of much strangeness,
I the juju man amongst you,
I have watched the strange pinnacles of birth, life, death,
All things pass.
The hand of God alone
Maps answers to all these miracles,
— In came Peter,
Without many words,
Only the fanaticism, the drive
The will that separates the genius, the man of destiny
From the lazy, the God-damned,
And damned-God-happy
Spades.
We reggae-happy, soul-happy
Betting-happy, sex-happy
Yea, very happy
Slaves.
— This blackman knew he was going to die,
Didn't he!
He knew we were basically cowards,
Didn't he!
He knew we'd kill, steal, curse each other blind
But do nothing,
Nothing to make ourselves independent of the white world,
Didn't he!
But in silence he fought for
Us.
In voice he cursed our stupidity,
In his short life,
Not one second hampered by the imminent death
He knew he held within him,
His achievements

Self-educated in their essence,
His school erected,
All his hard work condemns the work of us, the living
Blacks,
And says sadly that we will not soon
Find such another comet,
White man and black coward hater,
Noble, African warrior, lover, friend,
Our
Moses
To deliver us from the white pharoahs of
This white dominated planet,
The Pharoahs of our self-inflicting
Self-deceiving
Weaknesses,
To the truly high stature of
Our Black African destiny.

West-Indian Chaka

The first part of an unfinished epic.

Chained to the island rock, a Chaka bound
The African warrior surveys the
        shackled aspect of his fate
So late, yet not so long ago these chains,
Slavery's locks are fettered upon the mind.
The final fury,
Onslaught of the slave remains
Locked within the brain.
"The master is not killed,
Ever skattered[1] upon these rocks we are not free,
Oh why, oh why is all Africa
A cry of loss
A cry of pain!
Useless to plead the cause of
Black empires and glories long
Since passed
The brain demands an outlet
To this pain...
Betrayal is the cause,
The greed of chiefs
Grafted to the natural evil of the whites
Have strewn our black bodies
Wrecked us into both
Visual paradise and unearthly
Slavery upon these shores.
How, when and where shall a
West Indian Chaka rise?
Islands, all such small skattered
Tribes alone cannot raise us
To the level needed for self-atonement
From the past and present
Of black betrayal,
Upon white sin.
Could it be me that the
Waves so restlessly call

To pin my body to the cross of
Unnumbered, numberless
Black martyrs?
No it is not I.
Religion is one cause,
The causes of man another.
Overspiritualized for centuries
We blacks have called
To many of our genii
To mistake spirit for flesh,
And conjure our weak cowardice
As a whole, as evidence
Of nobility through the death of the individually noble".
The green foliage restlessly glissens,
Birds play tunes for insects,
The sun flirts its way through banana leaves:
Diffusion of sun-light, to green light
To darkness:
Diffusion, dislocation of Africa.
Nubian black, to brown,
Arab-mixed West African black
To creole blacks of the New World,
Diffusion, dislocation.
Breaking himself free from sheer
Natural arrogant and African strength,
The warrior severs his body from the rock.
Running again
As when in Africa by African
Hunted, to feed the belly
Of the slave ship.
Through forest, through the
Ironical mockery of a humming-bird's sweet chirp,
Deep into the mystic arms
Of the dark, tree-trunked forest
A runaway.
Satanic in its darkness
The forest gives genesis to
Foreboding thoughts:
"Memories of birth defamed
As a slave-sister's womb
Is cutlassed open,

Its fruit ejected and then crushed,
The insane nobility of those
Who threw themselves laughing into the sea,
While cowards such as I cowered the
Safety of our lives in shackles
Beneath the deck."
In a crescendo of despair,
Tears gushed from the runaway's face,
The whole being of the ancestor of original man
Shaken with the bleating tears of a child;
As if herself shaken in sympathy
The sky raged at this blasphemy
And pierced the sky with yellow thundersticks,
To prelude the sweeter sympathy of rain.
Enough, enough, of these barbarian tears,
What my mind has seen is beyond tears,
How can tears assuage the sell-out of black African
     brother
By black African brother.
The memory of death, hatred, the
Memory that is myself, the
Memory of being hunted,
The memory of rape,
That is myself.
The memory of blood mixing,
Of African, Amerindian, Indian
And European,
That is myself,
The memory of being branded. slave,
That is myself,
I the product of the sins of man,
I the product of betrayals,
What is there left for me
Except the necessity of revolt,
The necessity of total revolution.
And already, long ago, my brothers had begun,
Toussaint, Dessalines, Christophe,
For joy, for love of life,
The redemption of man, we left
One third of the army
Of that famous negro-hater, Napoleon,

Dead or defeated.
By the strength of Dahomean Voudoo
Insensed,
Oh this power, power of Africa within us,
Waiting, fighting, slowly but surely gaining
A means into the world.
In Jamaica by that blessed man Bogle
Led once more,
On an island where maroons in a world
White by colonialism, created a place
For the African, the now
West Indian, to stand.
On an island where nearly every day
My brothers, the West Indian
Sons of slaves have revolted,
And in these revolts have told the
Summary of their lives.
And what after all this blood,
What fruits can our minds boast of?
A little, you know we West Indians are a
Small nation,
Oh yes, a small nation of peasants,
Drunkards and crooked politicians,
Creole blacks, pure Africans,
Indians, Amerindians.
Somewhere in his soul the African
Despises us,
Everywhere in his soul the European hates us,
Somewhere in his soul the Chinaman
Despises us,
Yes, yes, no man can love us,
We West Indians,
We nothings,
We little people,
We the Educationally Subnormal,
We the "Nigger",
We the "Ajeweke",
We the "Son of Slaves",
We the "D'an Bawa",
We who gave Fanon to Africa,
We who gave Césaire to all African peoples,

We who gave Padmore to be poisoned[2] for love of
N'krumah's Ghana,
We who gave Blyden to help free Sierra Leone,
We who gave back Equiano for an end of slavery,
We who gave Garvey for our Black American brothers,
We who claim the Grenadian blood of Malcolm X,
We who claim Stokeley Carmichael as
A son of Trinidadian soil,
We who claim Belafonte as
A son of Bahamian soil,
We who claim that nigger actor Sidney Poitier as
A son of Bahamian soil,
And all our future sons,
For we are rich in thought,
As we are rich in ancestors,
As we are rich in history,
As we are rich in being by all peoples,
So much
Despised?
So what? Has it not always been so,
Have not the great always been
Despised,
We are part of a new West Indies,
As well as a new Africa,
And with enough N'krumahs,
With enough Lumumbas as our natural allies,
Our sons shall see further than even the moon,
We are the next creatures of destiny,
We are the next discoverers,
We are the next conquistadors,
We are the next inheritors of the earth,
It was our pact with the Lord of
The Universe in our Days of Slavery;
The destiny of all Sons of
Slaves
Is to become Sons of Masters.
The waves smash the shore,
The waves recede,
There is a little calm,
The waves start for their next conquest of the shore,
The rain, dying now of its former strength,

The tears of the new universal man,
The West Indian now assuaged,
The sun returns and calmly,
The plan of revolt, the plan of a new world,
Based on the African's powers of mind and body,
The past and present of his exploitation,
Based on the savage European's thirst for the
Blood of others and for conquest,
Based on the cannibal logic of the Carib
To survive one must eat others,
Based on the Indian's love of God and equal
Love of money,
Based on all this
This New African, this new tribe of Africa,
This West Indian king
Plans his conquest of the world.
What's this, what soft song
Now draws hatred from our young prince's heart:
What else but a woman's song:
The earth calls the sun,
The shore calls the sea,
Plants call for rain,
Man calls for woman.
A song, a song as soft as rain,
From all this discord made,
Form from chaos,
Sweet from bitter,
Found from loss,
Man begins again,
Forming his mission of barbarity and civilization:
"Uno love this place,
This place of de sun,
Uno love dis place o' rain.
De rain, de sun
De grass de grass
Blue blue de sky
Blue blue as well
De rivers and de sea,
Uno love dis place,
Dis place o' sea an' sun".
She sang she sang

As if the world were not
Made for care,
As if there was no beginning
Nor no end,
As if all war was made
To end in love,
As if all discord
Would forever end,
As if her song had made the world
Anew.
Stilled, shackeled by this
So sudden beauty,
Bolt still, a monk before a cross,
Transfixed and held, as if a humming-bird
Hovering before an unexpected flower,
Held up by nothing as it breaks its flight,
Except perhaps the sunray's strength
Which gilds it and transfigures it.
The warrior, fixed now
Before a woman's gaze,
Burning in the blaze of his eyes
A hard fusion of lust, love and adoration.
Bathing beneath the waterfall's sweet water
She was, musing, humming
In her soft dark-brown nakedness
She was, hallowed by a thousand crowns
Or sparkling droplets, on the softness of thick black hair,
She was, majesty in her movement,
Cat-like in her uncaring languish of her young body,
She was love on a summer's night,
She was the dark softness of the forest
Calling all those who entered her presence
To adore her.
All things in balance and imbalance, as nature ordered:
The young warrior imbalanced by his loneliness,
Imbalanced to credit such beauty
Its existence on the ugly world of man,
Imbalanced by lust,
Imbalanced by love,
Imbalanced by adoration,
He rushed to make her body inclusive to his thoughts.

1 Cf. scattered. The spelling used above is an attempt to refer to a Caribbean-like pronunciation of the word.

2.   Some Africans believe that Padmore was poisoned rather than died of natural causes in England.

Icare . . . Dédale[1]   Icarus . . .Dedalus[1]

Dans les cieux muets
Ou se pavane une belle mouette,
Icare; elle chante,
Dédale déscend,
Sur les dédales du vent . . .

Par les lèvres joyeuses
D'une belle Martiniquaise,
On attend le plaisir
Mais on quitte avec tristesse:
'Icare' ses lèvres,
'Dédale' ses seins,
'Icare!'
'Dédale!'
Je monte, je déscend,
Les plaisirs que je cherche,
L'amour qui m'échappe
— On monte!
— On déscend!
La lumière!
La distance! entre eux
— Ces deux
C'est notre éternité,
Notre vrai existence.

In the mute skies
Where a beautiful gull hovers,
Icarus; she cries,
Dedalus descends,
On the undulations of the wind . . .

Through the joyful lips
Of a beautiful girl from Martinique,
You await pleasure
But you leave with sadness:
'Icarus' her lips,
'Dedalus' her breasts,
'Icarus!'
'Dedalus!'
I rise, I fall,
The pleasures I search for,
The love that escapes me
— You rise!
— You fall!
The light!
The distance! between them
— These two
There is our eternity,
Our true existence.

---

1. A Greek myth about the wise Dedalus who constructs wings held
   together by wax and flies away from imprisonment, in contrast to
   his immature son Icarus who, not heeding his father's advice, flies
   too near the sun, resulting in the melting of the wax in his wings and
   thus his death.

Origins

Was it yesterday, tomorrow or today,
When he was taken?
Why are we always preyed on and
    oppressed?
Was it not good in fact that he was
    stolen and then sold?
If continuing old tactics
The white-skinned man-killers
Openly attacked again,
Surely we would all, like the
Red Indian,
Be but a people only in the
    memory of others?
Necessity, the old argument of our
Empires,
From Timbucktoo to Chad
Argued again its usefulness:
Better to have sold some slaves
So that we could live,
Some must always die
For others to live.

And what did we sell?
Was it not merely our rejects?
Criminals, intriguers against our
Just rulers,
The base born products of peasant
    wombs?
Prisoners of war,
Not our kin,
We merely sold strangers to strangers.
Yesterday and today is tomorrow;
Tomorrow perhaps it will
    all be forgotten,
No guilt can be ever truly

    said to be mine,
The kola nut in its sweetness
Must be paid for in the bitter foretaste
Of slaves.

III: Africa

Senegambia

Today and tomorrow and yesterday is now,
How long ago, how soon,
The same trees, the same beach,
The same incessant ocean.
Is it an ancestor that I make love to,
Is it an ancient enemy?
Welcome, and one is welcome,
Jama rèk,[1] and there is peace.
Today and tomorrow and yesterday is now
Am I on a West Indian beach?
Am I in Africa?
Today and tomorrow and yesterday is now,
Can I be born again
Or is no rebirth needed?
Is truth so simple that it requires no guise?
Is it all the question of non-questioned faith or its
    absence?
Talk not to me of Negritude as I have nothing more to
    prove.
Bloated as my blood is of every tribe, of every human
    race.
Oh free me free me from all tribal and some racial bonds,
My family is here and everywhere,
I am all the tribes, I am all the races.
But this freedom of thought this great expanse of the
    free heart,
Could it have been nurtured by anything else but Africa,
Who gave me my strength but Africa,
Who gave me my song but Africa,
Who bids me welcome but Africa,
Who like me is struggling to be free
But Africa?

---

1   A Wolof greeting meaning "Peace only".

Casamance River[1]

Was it upon your banks that I was slain,
Was it through these waters that I was dragged,
So cold, so cold, so grey,
Ancestor, answer me
For I can hear you.
Return to me another voice stronger than despair:
Arm me, arm me, let me hear defiance,
Let me hear revenge,
Let me hear plots bounded in chains,
Let me hear the
Instruments by which I must ensure our future.
I cannot make my peace amongst your cries
Allah Wakbar,[2] Jesus, Jesus,
They enslaved you
And now they ask for peace, for forgetfulness,
To be forgiven and even loved!
Oh ancestor chained on the boat,
Poured out on this river mouth,
How can you be at peace
While I am in invisible chains?

---

1 A river in southern Senegal through which slaves were shipped to
the Caribbean.
2 Meaning "There is no God but God", being one of the pillars of
faith of Islam.

Gorée

They tell me you have made men cry,
They tell me your chains frighten them.
They say oh the crime, the woe, the sighs
Of guilt of the present ancestors of those who built you.
But how can I be frightened of you
When I am the produce of your
Womb.
I will come back to see you one day,
But only to shout and loudly laugh:
You tried to kill me once,
It was tried by masters at the art
But for myself and all my tribe I cry
I am still here,
I'm here!
I'm here!
But where are you?

1   Gorée is an off-shore island close to Dakar, on the Senegalese coast
    where slaves were kept before shipment to slave plantations in
    America and the Caribbean.

For Loulou Gomes

My brother's eyes move like a cat,
My brother calculates everything,
Quick, lithe, a master of subtlety,
A gentle and a loving man
Metamorphosed by experience into a more lasting mould.
What gave you that sharp and careful mental grace,
My brother?
Is it the condition of life in Africa?
Does grace, does goodness, all,
Only by subtlety survive here?
Or is this your God's gift,
This mind that dances over figures,
Outcalculates figures, men, perhaps even itself?
My brother's mind moves like a panther.

For a Rastaman Met in Senegambia

Locks-man of peace
Moved to war,
Gentility forced to aggression,
Art moved to war,
Picture of our history this
Brown locks upon light-brown skin.
Something has happened,
Something has happened...
An ancestor cried out from here for your return,
A picture of our history you are
Of all the strength and desolation that is loss,
Moving back to the ancestral womb
To reforge itself into an even finer steel,
My brother they all came
From North from South
From East and West,
From inside
To make us slaves,
Instead they created
Supermen.

Song of a Return to Babylon

Mother, African mother,
I am going again
To dark lands,
To sad faces
And all of nature's inelegancies,
Again, again to an absence of myself.
Mother, when I leave
Come with me,
Send the spirits of my ancestors
To shield me,
But hold part of my soul here
Till my return.
I have travelled far and long with
Only your image as my strength.
I have travelled far and long,
With only the image of your absence,
But I have to go again.
A warrior's life is not his own,
And you did not raise us
To run from any fight.
So I will go again
Knowing I will return,
That my success is your success
And that forever we are one.

Re-Exiled: Nigeria

Grains of endless sand,
The desert encroaches,
The dust of what was
Or might have been.

Flies encroach,
Cold, hot without and
With harmattan[i].

Silence, dust.
A grain of sand upon
A grain of sand.

Exiled once
A son of slaves,
A dust from one heap
Piled upon another heap.

Exiled twice,
Babylon's whore
Called for willing labour:
Prostitutes calling prostitutes.
We came, we saw,
We were reconquered.

Back again,
A dust returns to dust.
Returns to flies
And a black prostitute.

Whore who kills her
Children living.
Murderess,
Killing even the
Foetus of her creation.

Exiled, exiled once,
Exiled twice.
Returning to find,
Minds based
On permanent mental exile.

Mercedes is king,
The whorehouses are full,
The rumshop, self-suicide,
Replaced by the beerclubs,
And the fat opulence of
Suicidal consumers:
Grown men with soft
Women's hands.

Dust returns to dust,
Exiles return to exiles.

---

1 A dry desiccating wind usually associated with dust and lower
   temperatures in Northern Nigeria.

Enspiwasyon   Inspiration

The heavens ache,
All the songs that might have been,
Lightening blue,
With thunder's cry,
Blue to touch,
Blue plunder of the earth.

But they were not sung,
The blue did not touch.
Heart-ache of colonial slavery
Voices held in prison,
Prisoners holding in an ache.

The cry is all around.
And you cannot escape
To blue clouds,
To calm seas,
To deep philosophy
Here where philosophy
Here where philosophy is action.

Mwen té pé palé
Men yo tjwé vwa mwen.
Mwen té vlé volé
Men yo koupé sél mwen.
Lang mwen ka bat sèlman
Kon kutum, kon tjè mwen.

Ki tan ki tan vwa-a
Kai viwé.
Jibyé blé èspwa,
Cyèl blé lapé,
San tonnè, san zéklè,
Men épi zyé klè.

Déviwé an jou ti bèl péyi,
Bèl péyi èspwa,
Déviwé an jou bèl vwa,
Déchenen mwen,
Libéwé tèt mwen.

I could have spoken
But they killed my voice.
I wanted to fly
But they cut my wings.
My tongue only beats
Like a habit, like my heart.

When oh when will the voice
return.
The blue bird of hope,
The blue sky of peace,
Without thunder, without lightening
But with clarity.

Return again one day the
beautiful country,
Beautiful country of hope.
Return again beautiful voice,
Unchain me,
Liberate my head.

Kité mwen sav ankò	Let me know again
Difé katjil	The fire of thought,
Kité mwen sav ankò	Let me know again
Katjil èk aksyon,	Thought with action,
Ansam, ansam,	Together, together,
Blé tonnè,	Blue thunder,
Blé plézi	Blue pleasure
Enspiwasyon.	Inspiration.

Gwo Piton Pitit Piton

Tjèk fwa adan lavi
Lavi ka ba nou wòch,
Lavi ka ba nou fè.

Tjèk fwa adan nan vi,
Wòch ka pété douvan jyé'w,
Fè nan difé cho lavi ka kwazé'w,

Men chonjé:
Sé woch asou wòch
ka fè gwo piton, piti piton,
Difé asou difé Ka fè gwo piton sòti piti piton.

Mòn lavi ki nou ka monté,
Ban nou fè nan tjè,
Wòch lavi nou ka pléwé,
Ban nou difé nan tjè.

Gwo piton piti piton,
Antwé nan tjè-nou.
Kité nou défan sa Kawayib
Défan ban-nou.
Wòch lavi, difé lavi.
Gwo Piton, Piton nou la! Nou la!
Gwo Piton, Piton nou la! Nou la!
Gwo Piton, Piti Piton . . . . . .
Gwo Piton, Piti Piton . . . . .

Large Piton Small Piton

Sometimes in life
life gives us stones,
Life gives us iron.

Sometimes in a life,
Stones burst before your eyes,
Iron in the hot fire of life crushes you.

But remember:
It is stone upon stone
Which makes the large *piton* the small *piton,* Fire upon
fire which makes the large *piton* emerge from the small *Piton.*

Mountainsof life that we climb,
Give us iron in the heart,
Stones of life that we cry of,
Give us fire in the heart.

Large *Piton* small *piton,*
Enter our hearts,
Let us defend what Caribs
Defended for us.
Stones of life fires of life,
Gwo Piton, Piti Piton we are here! We are here!
Gwo Piton, Piti Piton we are here! We are here!
Gwo Piton, Piti Piton . . . . .
Gwo Piton, Piti Piton . . . . .

---

1.   In the south-west of St. Lucia (The Caribbean) there are two volcanic hills which
rise almost vertically from the sea. The larger hill is called *Gwo Piton* and the smaller
hill, *Piti Piton.* The descendants of the St. Lucian Carib are to be found in the areas
near *Gwo Piton* and *Piti Piton.*

Misifan Grenada

Sun zo su kakashe mu
Ba ruwa,
Sun ce wai za ma fad'a musu da fad'a.
Ina an ga
'Dan tsako ke hana zakara abinci?

Ba abin da Ladan[1] ya fad'a tun da da?
Ba had'a kai, had'a kai kan nema?
Amma, har yanzu
Taskaninmu mu ke son fad'a.
Ashe ko k'ananan dabobi ke tsoron giwa,
Sun fi son kashe kansu.

Yaya Bishop, Allah ya ji kansa,
Yaya? Yaya
Kai da Coard kun fara fad'a?
Ba kun riga kun sani?
Giwa ke jira,
Ke alla alla ya kashe ku,
Da maganarsa: ku wajen ni ku nama,
In zama kunama wajenku.

Har yanzu,
Tun Afrika mun fara da irin banza:
Filani ba ya son Bamaguje,
Mai arewa ba ya son mai kudu,
Mai tudu ba ya son mai fili.
Ashe tun da da can muna haka,
Muna tonen kaburburanmu.

Allah, yau da gobe,
Ka ilmantad da halayenmu,
Ka fisshe mu da
Irin zaman dabbanmu.

The Tragedy of Grenada

They came to kill us
Without a reason,
They say we intended to attack them.
Where has one seen
A chick stop a cock from eating?

Is this not what Ladan[1] said long ago?
Is it not unity, unity that we seek?
But, right up to today
Between us we love to quarrel.
Indeed although smaller animals fear the elephant,
They prefer to kill each other.

How on earth Bishop, God rest his soul,
How on earth? How on earth?
Did you and Coard begin to fight?
Did you not already know?
The elephant waits,
Is hoping might and main to kill you,
From his very words:
As far as I'm concerned you are meat
Let me be the scorpion towards you.

Right up to today,
Since Africa we began this stupidity:
The Fulani does not like the Bamaguje,
The northerner does not like the southerner,
Those living in the hills do not like those on the plains.
Indeed since long ago over there we were thus,
We've been digging our graves.

Dear God, as time goes on,
Enlighten our character,
Deliver us from our life of beasts.

Ka nuna wa kowa,
Ko a zuciyar farin mutum,
Ko a zuciyar bakin mutum,
Kai ne mai kashewa,
Kai ne mai gyarawa.
Ka taimake mu 'yan Afrika,
Ko a Afrika, ko a tsibaran Wiskindiya,
Ka nuna mana,
Da son kanmu za mu ci gaba,
In ba wannan so,
Kome siyarsa, ba gyarawa.
Da son aikinsa,
Mai d'inkin hular ke kyaun aiki,
Da son kanmu,
Za mu taimaki kanmu.

---

1. Hausa singer of *Had'a Kai Afrika* — Africa Unite.

Show everyone,
Whether in the heart of the white man,
Or in the heart of the black man,
You are the bringer of death,
You are the repairer.
Help us the sons and daughters of Africa,
Whether in Africa or in the Caribbean islands,
Show us,
That by loving ourselves we shall advance,
Without such love,
No matter what political system, there will be no cure.
By loving his work,
The sewer of hats makes beautiful hats,
By loving ourselves,
We shall help ourselves.

Mwen Palé Bay Tig

Mwen palé bay Tig,
Tig gwondé ban mwen.
Mwen di Tig, "Misyé,
Pouchi ou emen
Lapen kon èlslav?"

"Lapen, lavéwité
Istava sé sa:
Zòt sé moun tèlman
Dous.
Zòt sé moun tèlman
Wich.
Zòt sé moun
Épi tèlman èspwi" . . .

"Pouchi misyé Tig?
Pouchi'w vlé tchwé
Moun tèlman bon kon nou?"

"Lapen, si mwen manjé dousè,
Mwen kay vini dous.
Si mwen manjé wichès,
Mwen kay vini wich.
Si mwen manjé èspwi,
Mwen kay ni lèspwi."

"Men Konpè Tig,
Ki sa nou fè 'w?
Ki sa nou fè 'w?
Pou fè'w tchwé nou?"

"Lapen, Lapen,
Menm malen,
Ki'w malen,
Ès ou pòkò ka kopwan?
Sé kon ha mwen ka viv?"

I Spoke to Tiger

I spoke to Tiger,
Tiger grumbled to me.
I told Tiger, "Mister,
Why do you love
Keeping Rabbits as slaves?"

Rabbit, the truth of
The story is this:
You are people who are so
Good natured.
You are people who are so
Rich.
You are people who
Have so much intelligence . . ."

"Why mister Tiger?
Who do you want to kill
People as good as us?"

"Rabbit if I eat sweetness,
I will become sweet.
If I eat richness,
I will become rich.
If I eat intelligence,
I will gain intelligence.

"But brother Tiger,
What have we done you?
What have we done you?
To make you kill us?"

"Rabbit, my dear Rabbit,
Even as wily,
As you are wily,
Can you still not understand?
That's how I live?"

Batay Kòk

Cock Fight

Kòk shanté: Non mwen Bishop!
Kòk shanté: Non mwen sé Coard!
Kòk shanté: Non mwen Reagan!

The cock sings: My name is Bishop!
The cock sings: My name is Coard!
The cock sings: My name is Reagan!

Bishop: Gwaté, gwaté
           Pou manjé nou,
           Gwaté, gwaté
           Pou lavi nou,
           San gwan Ajablés
           Méwichen vini
           Gwaté nou èk
           Manjé nou!

Bishop: Scratch, scratch
           For our food,
           Scratch, scratch
           For our lives,
           Without the large
           Yankee Adjables[1]
           Scratching us, and
           Eating us!

Coard: Gwaté, gwaté
           Pou manjé nou,
           Gwaté, gwaté
           Pou èdikasyon nou.
           Twavay, twavay,
           Sèlman twavay.

Coard: Scratch, scratch
           For our food
           Scratch, scratch
           For our education.
           Work, work,
           Only work.

Reagan: Tchwé, tchwé!
           Wavèt pa ni wézon
           Douvan poul!
           Ni poul, ni nom
           Pan ni wezon
           Douvan mwen!

Reagan: Kill, kill!
           The cockroach has no right
           In front of the chicken!
           Neither chickens nor men
           Have any rights
           Before me!

           San èk zo sé manjé mwen
           Mwen sé gonslinger!
           Mwen sé Adjablès!
           Mwen sé mové
           Tchenbwa,
           Mwen sé bolom
           Lamen mèt gajé.

           Blood and bones are my food
           I am a gunslinger!
           I am an Adjables!
           I am bad magic,
           I am the unborn child
           Bolom[2], servant of
           The master witchdoctor.

           San èk zo sé manjé mwen.
           Asou bèl kwis poul
           Mwen ka viv.
           Kité yo gwaté,
           Kité yo twavay,
           Kité yo vin gwa
           Èk lè kò yo lis,
           Lè kò yo gwa,
           Lè yo ni tan
           Djwé batay kòk
           Pami kò yo.

           Blood and bones are my food.
           On the beautiful thighs of
           chickens I live.
           Let them scratch,
           Let them work,
           Let them become fat
           And when their bodies are smooth,
           When their bodies are fat,
           When they have time
           For cock fights
           Amongst themselves.

           Sé la, ha! ha! ha!
           Sé la, ha! ha! ha!
           Sé la, ha! ha! ha!
           Mwen kay tchwé yo!

           It's then, ha! ha! ha!
           It's then, ha! ha! ha!
           It's then, ha! ha! ha!
           I will kill them!

1.   A woman with one cloven hoof who, in Patwa mythology, entices men to jump over precipices in their bids to gain her favours.
2.   An invisible dwarf created by master herbalists in Saint Lucia, through taking the unborn foetus from the womb of a mother and making it their invisible servant..

To a Brother

In a different world
My brother,
I would say,
Marry whoever you like:
Chinese, Javanese, European ...
Are we not all children
Of one universal
Creator?
But in this world
Where Blacks are universally
Unequal,
I would be afraid
Of beating my white wife
After being refused too many
Jobs
Because of colour.
Worse still
I would be afraid,
After watching Blacks
Daily murdered
In South Africa,
Starved by international conspiracy
In Ethiopia,
I would like Othello want
To put out that White
And terrible light!

To a Sister

In a different world
My sister,
I would say
Marry whoever you like:
Chinese, Javanese, European ...
Are we not children of one universal
Creator?
But, why is it that
Like your brother before
You chose to marry
Only from the
Gutters of Europe?
Not even Europe's palaces?
The whites we marry,
For some strange reason,
Must always be
Less intelligent than us,
Poorer than us,
Uglier than us.

Have we been so long
Oppressed
That we cannot even hope
Or reach out for the best?

Or is it that slavery
Has not ended,
And you still feel the itch
For massah bed?

For Those Who Have Become Goyim [1]

I mourn your loss
I rip my cloth
I dry
The unshed tears from my
Eyes.

We have Goyim's
Clothes
We have Goyim's
Machines
We have Goyim's
Language
Yes!

But we are
Not Goyim.

Who will put out
Food on
The graves of your
Ancestors?

Who will make
The link
For you
Between the living
And the dead?

I cry for the
Spirits of your
Ancestors.
Who will not be able
To get even
Libations of water,
Or even spit,

From the lips
Of your pale
Descendants.

I will go to the
Graves of my
Slave ancestors
Whole.
I will face them
Whole.
We will speak
Whole.
We will speak
Without apologies.

I will move
Out from my present
History
And create
My own machines,
My own clothes
My own language.

I will be a
Creator,
And not a beggar,
On the face of
God's earth.

I continue
To give food
To the spirits
Of my ancestors.
I continue to
Give libations
Of blood
Wine
Rum
And water

To their
Spirits.
May my lips continue
To give them their
Poetry.

May our children
Know our thoughts,
And choose to
Join us.

May we make
Peace amongst
Ourselves,
Before we attempt
World peace.

May we make
Love amongst
Ourselves,
Before we attempt
World love.

He loveth best
Who first can love
Himself.

Keep me free
From Satanic Goyim
Gods
Who wish me
To love internationally
But hate at
Home,
For Marx's, Christ's, the Dollar's
Or some other's sake.

Let me find peace
With my fellow slaves: Caribbeans,
Black Americans and Africans.

If we can manage that in
Truth and not hypocracy,
Then there can be peace with
Goyim.

----

1. A Yiddish word meaning 'outsiders', 'non-Jews'

For Those Who Will Come After

For those who will come after:
We offer you our dreams,
We offer you our loss,
We offer you our joy,
We offer you our pain.

For those who will come after,
Be stronger than we were,
Dream higher than we dreamt,
Go further than we went.

For those who will come after,
Beware their world of death,
Beware their world without a heart.
Trust not their lies,
They tell them often.
Trust only in ourselves.
Create the uncreated self
The uncreated man.

Pity not our enemies within,
They feed like vultures
Upon our deaths.
Stop not, where they tell us
To stop.

Search on and onward, forever
Create and uncreate,
Continue and continue
To create.

We the blessing
Of the unblessed,
We the offering
For those who will come after.

Claim not no peace for self
Claim not no rest.

Live on, live on through
Time,
And in time.
African
Ancestor and descendant:
Create!
Create!
Onward and forever,
For those who will come after.